SCOTLAND FOR BEGINNERS
Bannockburn an' a' that

Rupert Besley

NEIL WILSON PUBLISHING
Glasgow · Scotland

Published by Neil Wilson Publishing Ltd
309 The Pentagon Centre, 36 Washington St
Glasgow G3 8AZ
Tel: 041-221 1117   Fax: 041-221 5363
First published in 1990 by
Lochar Publishing, Moffat

A catalogue record for this book is available from
the British Library

ISBN 1-897784-00-7

Typeset in 9/10pt Bodoni by
Hewer Text Composition Services, Edinburgh
and printed in Great Britain by
Scotprint Ltd in Musselburgh

CONTENTS

Arrival

Crossing the Border – Greetings and Common Expressions

WELCOME TO SCOTLAND!

Gang awa', gang awa', gang awa'
Shav' aff, git oot, gang awa'
Trad. Border Ballad

Make no mistake about it, you'll never forget the welcome you receive when you cross into Scotland. The Scots are famous for it.

For as long as folk can remember, Scotland has been invaded by eager hordes each summer, keen to enjoy the scenery and sample the hospitality. When Edward I journeyed north with his caravan all those years ago, little can he have imagined what a precedent he was setting for future generations. The people of Scotland have been chucking out the welcome mats and laying on suitable reception parties for his successors ever since.

WELCOME TO SCOTLAND

ARRIVAL IN SCOTLAND:
A FEW SIMPLE DO'S AND DON'TS

Crossing the Border from England can be a lengthy and trying process. Visitors are strongly advised to make preparations where possible in advance of their journey, in order to cut down on delays at border check-points.

Simple measures that can be taken at any time of year include the pre-stamping of passports or temporary visas (just pop into your local Passport Office or Scottish Embassy), the exchange of appropriate currency through your bank (Scottish Poonds are usually available straight across the counter), the purchase of a phrase-book and basic groceries and, of course, the addition of snow-chains to the wheels of your car (advisable, though not yet obligatory in most parts of Scotland).

Once you have passed the quick medical check-up and got over the more rigorous written exam imposed by the Scottish Tourist Board, you will be safely through the border-controls and free to continue your journey north – keeping a watchful eye out from this moment on for Arctic Hare, Golden Eagles and Red Deer by the roadside.

N.B. Don't forget that in Scotland you always drive in the MIDDLE of the road.

MAKING YOURSELF UNDERSTOOD

As in any foreign country, the locals will appreciate your efforts to join in their language with appropriate usage of common phrases – aye, nae, och, wee, the noo etc.

Here are some further everyday greetings and common expressions that you may care to practise:–

Jock	Sir
Hinnie	Madam
Hoozyersel?	How do you do?
Whit'll ye hae?	Allow me
Nae borra	My pleasure
Dinna fash yersel	No, thank-you
Haud yer wheesht!	Excuse me!
Dinna ken	Could you repeat that?

TOURIST TIP

To pronounce the Scottish 'ch' sound (as in 'loch', 'wee doch'n doris', 'What's up, doch?' etc.), place one half-stick of freshly cut celery (4¾ ins. long) in the mouth, at right angles to the tongue, and stand well back from those you wish to converse with.

In summer months rhubarb may be used instead.

View down Loch Tay

Geography

Location – Regions – Maps – Geology – Climate

i) SCOTLAND: WHERE IS IT?

For as long as history records, it has been the aim of successive governments to fade out Scotland, a bold objective which has come close to achievement on a number of occasions, thanks to long spells of low clouds rolling in from the west and to the wiles of generations of civil servants employed by the Ordnance Survey, the AA etc. (see maps below) –

Scots have only recently been able to gain a true perspective on their place in the world, thanks largely to the generous efforts of a former American astronaut, keen to prove his Scottish ancestry, who managed to smuggle into Leith highly sensitive satellite pictures of Britain from space. The famous Scotsat snaps, preserved in Edinburgh Castle, form the basis of the Revised McPeters' Projection, shown below.

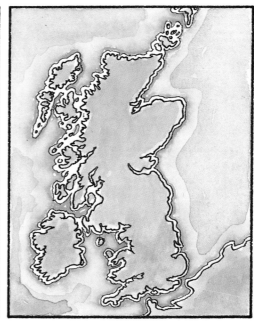

ii) THE REGIONS

Scotland has more or less managed to retain its basic shape, despite local boundary changes leading, for example, to the loss of Kincardine and Peebles. It is still possible to think of Scotland falling into two parts basically, Glasgow and The Rest.

For purposes of administration and collection of the poll tax, Scotland is divided into 12 regions, each with its own distinctive charm and character. These are listed below, together with places which are compulsory stops for the tourist in each area –

BORDERS – Scott's View, glimpsed from the hearse on his final journey.

DUMFRIES & GALLOWAY – Gretna Green, where generations of under-age English newly-weds consummated their marriage over the anvil.

STRATHCLYDE – Spanish Armada galleon in Tobermory Bay.

GLASGOW – Haggis Castle.

EDINBURGH – 'Lands' – tall tenement buildings (kind of early time share) which take their name from the cry that came when the contents of a chamber-pot scored a direct hit in the street below.

LOTHIAN – painters on the Forth Bridge.

CENTRAL – Bannockburn, the main event in Scottish History, when Bruce, fielding a side severely understrength, inflicted a crushing defeat on the English team well before half-time.

KINGDOM OF FIFE – Changing the Guard-Dogs before the Royal and Ancient Golf Club at St Andrews.

TAYSIDE – Manufacture of Caithness Glass near Perth, before it sets out on its precarious journey north.

GRAMPIAN – Tour of whishky distillerilleries.

HIGHLANDS – Glencoe Chairlift (take cushions and the usual air travel precautions).

ORKNEY & SHETLAND – see mainland Norway on a clear day.

80% of the population of Scotland lives in a 4 large towns (except in August, when anyone with any sense gets out of Edinburgh). Glasgow is the culture centre of Scotland, while Edinburgh (Auld Reekie) has long been the home of heavy industry.

Scots are divided into two sorts, Highlanders and Lowlanders, according to their height.

Small islands make up the bulk of Scotland and these range from the tomato-shaped Ailsa Craig in the south to Iceland in the north.

The Highlands were emptied in the 19th century.

SOME SCOTTISH-PLACE NAMES EXPLAINED

Highlands	– probably derived from the Old Norse word 'hoy' (pronounced 'hoy') meaning 'High'.
Sutherland	– in the far north, means 'South-er-land'.
Dun	– castle, as in Dunvegan, Dunnottar, Dunromin.
Inver-	– mouth of.
Peterhead	– head of Peter.
Arthur's Seat	– characteristically rounded knoll.
Muckle	– big.
Muckle Flugga	– big Flugga.
Mor	– big.
Biggar	from 'beg' meaning 'little'.

View down Loch Rannoch

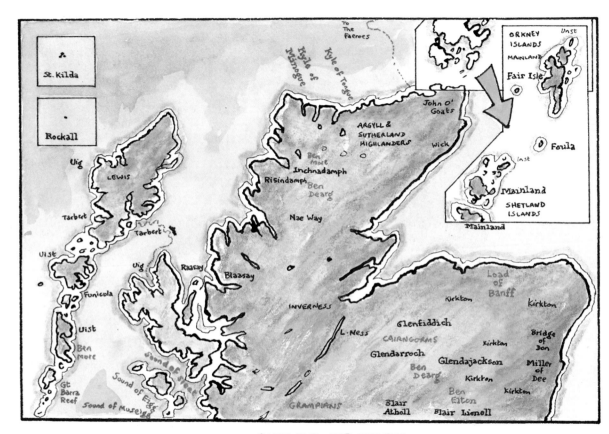

SCOTLAND: THE TOP BIT

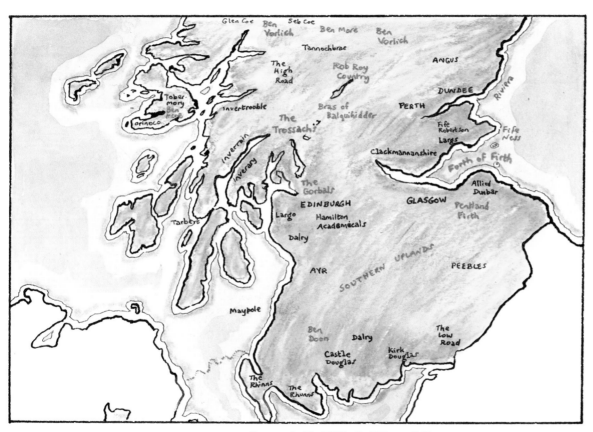

SCOTLAND·THE BOTTOM BIT

iv) SOME NOTES ON GEOLOGY

Scotland has the oldest rock in Britain, proving once and for all that Scotland got here first. The north-west corner of Scotland consists mostly of old volcanoes (naughty, but gneiss). This region, made up of black gabbro, formica and schist, is a geologist's paradise with such notable sights as Fingal's Cave, where the lava-flows cooled into extraordinary configurations of Edinburgh Rock.

The rest of Scotland is cut off by faults and still in the throes of Glacial Movements. It is the smoothing effect of the ice-sheet that is responsible for the perfect shaping of the Paps of Jura; likewise a number of other tall mountains in Scotland, known as the Marilyn Monroes.

No less remarkable (and still from the Plasticine Era) are the 'parallel roads' around Glen Roy, much celebrated in song ('O, you'll tak the high road . . .').

Scotland has two great lakes (or 'lochs'), Loch Lomond and Loch Ness, and a great many others with unpronounceable names.

Most of Scotland consists of islands. There are more than 500 of these, ranging from windswept, treeless Coll in the west to the lush, wooded slopes of the Black Isle in the east; from the bogs of Lewis to the semi-alpine scenery of Jura and the Vosges.

Between these extremes lies an intricate jigsaw of interlocking land-masses, neatly connected by bridges at strategic points (Bridge of Allan, Bridge of Orchy etc.).

Treeless Coll . . .

HOW THE BASS ROCK WAS FORMED: A RECENT THEORY

FINGAL'S CAVE IN STAFFS, INSPIRATION FOR ONE OF MENDELSSOHN'S BIGGEST HITS

'WE'RE OUT OF WATER!'

Winters in Scotland
can be harsh...

v) THE WEATHER

Scotland has lots of weather, much of it varied and interesting. The weather in Scotland has been the butt of many a joke – often quite unfairly, as the Scottish climate is considerably more reliable than elsewhere: it always rains on Public Holidays.

Winters in Scotland can be harsh, but not everywhere. While the East Coast may be flattened by bitterly cold winds that scream through the Urals, the frost-free, palm-fringed West Coast may be basking in warmth brought over by the Gulf Stream. This explains why Aberdonians tend to face west in winter.

Spring brings the promise of sunshine and new warmth to clear away the winter snows. This usually happens by the third week in March.

(N.B. DATE FOR YOUR DIARY: Mar 14–20
Snow Fun Week in Glenshee.)

Summers in Scotland are hot and sunny, as elsewhere, but sometimes disappointingly short, lasting perhaps just one day or two. However, it is always sunny on Tiree, by day and by night, and pessimists would do well to reflect upon the fact that Dundee could not have built up its world-wide reputation for marmalade without receiving a modicum of sunshine each year to ripen the oranges.

Fact: In June 1971 the island of Tiree averaged 256 hours of sunshine a day.

Autumn in Scotland is always a delight. This is the best season for mists, nature's way of adding lace-curtains to the view. But there is always one day each autumn when the skies clear as if by magic. This is an important day for Scots all round the world, as photographers from far and wide speed over to Loch Duich to capture the castle of Eilean Donan for next year's calendars.

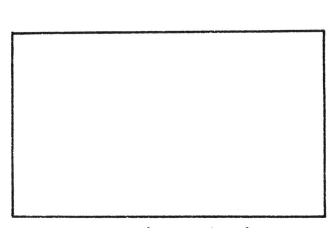

The View from the top of
Ben Nevis

Natural History

Flora, Fauna, Feathered Friends – A Great Painter

FEATHERED FRIENDS

From the shy greeting of the bashful Bonxie perched on its clifftop lookout to the delicate flit of the diminutive capercaillie among the slender branches of the Ancient Caledonian Forest, Scotland has much to thrill the serious ornithologist.

Spring and autumn are of course the best times of year to watch the passage of great flocks of bird-lovers on their seasonal migrations. But the patient observer may be rewarded by the sight of a nesting twitcher at almost any time of year.

GANNETS ON AILSA CRAIG

A correspondent writes:

Against a sky of beaten lead the chevron skeins of greylag come whiffling down the dark, drool glen. A roding woodcock tharbles on the brae. A quiver 'mongst the copper fronds: the long-nebbed curlew nestles in the coverlet of asphodel and myrtle. Past the staring roebuck springs the lively sheep-tick etc. etc.

21

JOURNEY'S END FOR THE SPAWNING SALMON

WEE
SLEEKIT
COW'RIN'
TIM'ROUS
BEASTIE

Amang the blooming heather
— Burns

Naturists all over the world are attracted to Scotland for its Wild Life.

Reindeer, eagles, moose ('Wee, sleekit, cow'rin', tim'rous beastie' – Burns), otter, midge – Scotland has them all in plenty, and, thanks to careful management of resources, the authorities have made it possible for threatened species to flourish again. One of Scotland's great success-stories has been the return of the ostrich to Loch Garten.

Who could deny the thrill of watching the ptarmigan change its colours or the simple pleasure to be had from the sweet music of the gannetry? What a joy it is to see the Golden Eagle land on the bird-table or to witness the arrival of barnacles on Isla St. Clair.

22

Heather on the hillsides, lovely Flora spread out on the machair; dolphins basking off the foreshore, forests teeming with wildcat and pine-marten; footpaths carpeted with cloudberry, thistle and furze . . . the lover of nature is spoilt for choice.

But for the many visitors the greatest excitement is to be had from spotting deer, easily seen browsing in herds on upper slopes all over Scotland. (Do remember, though, that deer do not have big udders and go moo.)

Newcomers are often surprised to find that large tracts of land marked 'Deer Forest' on the map are in fact completely devoid of trees, such is the deer's natural voracity for timber. However, with careful planting schemes (many of them financed by famous names from screen and stage), the Forestry Commission and other agencies have done much in recent years to encourage the deer back into Scotland.

'LOOK – A SEAL!'

A GREAT PAINTER?

Many visitors, reared on 'The Monarch of the Glen', are often disappointed to discover that the red deer does not in fact tower over the rest of Creation from a height of 10 or 15 feet. However, recent studies in perspective analysis at the University of Strathclyde have led one critic to suggest that Sir Edwin Landseer may have been no more than 1ft. 9ins. tall at the time of completing his famous oeuvre. (What cannot be denied is Landseer's remarkable abilities as a deerstalker, having had to approach his model each day by crawling long distances on his belly through the heather, bearing palette and canvas in his teeth, unnoticed all the way – in this at least, his small stature may have been of some advantage to him.)

Finally, a word on conservation. Scotland has a rich heritage of rare species: the Orkney vole, Shetland pony, Loch Fyne kipper, Soay sheep, Rhum truffle, Scottish primrose, Scotch thistle (found only in E. Anglia) . . . Many of these endangered species, like the Highland mole, have an uphill struggle, needing always to adapt in order to survive. Such a creature is the St Kilda Mouse, living on in abject isolation; it feeds mainly on fulmar and gannet, but dreams only of cheese.

LIFE CAN BE TOUGH FOR THE HIGHLAND MOLE

ON THE TRAIL OF THE ELUSIVE WILDCAT

Royal Scotland

Kings, Queens & John Brown

Kings and queens have long been accorded a special place in Scotland; 48 of them are buried on Iona.

The close relationship that exists between Scotland and the monarchy is something that has been forged over the centuries, but which gained a special significance during the long rain of Queen Victoria.

THE ROYAL PARTY OUT DEER-STALKING. 1859.

Scotland has had a great many famous kings and queens and some pretenders.

It was Kenneth Macalpine the Builder who started the whole thing rolling, when he picked up a large stone at Scone, which he promptly dropped. This became the famous Dropped Scone of Stone, on which all future kings and queens were crowned. These included a great many called James and one called Mary, who married the sickly Dolphin. After union difficulties the James' took on dual registration numbers to add to the confusion.

The strong links with Scotland maintained by our present Royal Family owe much to the wanderings of Victoria and Albert in the Highlands. After Albert's untimely death, John Brown was summoned urgently from his shipyards over to Balmoral to cheer up the Queen, a difficult task in which he was brilliantly successful.

THE QUEEN'S VIEW 1860

THE QUEEN'S VIEW 1862

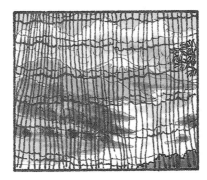

A new method of deerstalking on trial in the Highlands
of Scotland.

History

A brief survey from earliest times

In the beginning Scotland's only inhabitants were a small group of people living underground on Orkney. This was the Stone Age and life was generally uncomfortable until the arrival of the Beaker Folk.

The Dark Ages continued for many centuries with few chinks of light at the end of the tunnel. However, there was plenty of new land to be had as the ice-sheets retreated, property was cheap and Scotland succumbed to hordes of monosyllabic invaders, like Celts and Picts and Gaels. Little is known about these early folk, who built large Brooches and the Ring of Brodgar.

One for the Wood –

When the Romans came along, they were defeated by the Scottish landscape in their attempts to build straight roads, so they put a wall across the A1 and M6, which shut off Scotland for several centuries. Around this time, pious Antoninus speaks of Picts who painted themselves blue, but they may just have been feeling the cold.

Skipping on ahead past Macbeth, Macduff and all the Witches, we come to a better-known chapter in Scottish affairs, featuring Wallace Wha' Hae', the Scots Wham, Bruce and the Spider.

ROMAN IN THE GLOAMIN

On to the glorious reign of Mary, Queen of Scots, whose husband Darning came to blows with Rizzio, the Italian secretary. They murdered each other over supper and Mary married Boswell instead. This set her off on a life of tragic wandering, in which she spent one dismal night in every castle in Britain, until she got to Fotheringay, where she nobly submitted to the executioner's axe, with Cally engraved on her heart.

At this point Scottish History enters a distinctly gloomy patch, unrelieved till the appearance of Rob Roy. Against a dark background of clan-feuding and cattle-theft, Bonnie Prince Charlie landed on Skye to rally the clans round the monument at Glenfinnan. The rest is history.

Athens of the North

On a happier note, Scotland had a brief burst of glory in the 18th century, when the sun came out in Edinburgh and much was achieved in architecture, philosophy and copying bits of the Parthenon. These developments came to a tragic halt with the Tay Bridge Disaster in 1879.

Efforts were made to cheer up the people, but life in Scotland continued to be grim, particularly in the cities where mounting unemployment gave rise to cholera, clapshot and frequent nasty injuries in the gorbals. However, all this was changed in recent times by the creation of the Glasgow Garden Festival and the discovery of oil in the North Sea.

The discovery of oil in the North Sea...

'HEBRIDES, MALIN, IRISH SEA – HERE IS AN URGENT GAEL WARNING – '

Clans & Tartans

The Clan System – Highland Dress

THE CLAN SYSTEM

The word 'clan' comes from the Gaelic 'clann', meaning offspring, tribe or clan.

The Clan System was introduced in the 11th century and was essentially a bureaucratic measure, whereby the population of Scotland was split up by surname and people with the same name were required to live together in alphabetical order. Thus were forged the strong links between the clans and their territories – Stuarts and Bute, Macdonells and Glengarry, Macbraynes and the Islands. All this did create some difficulties for the postman, but did at least make family get-togethers at Christmas relatively simple to arrange.

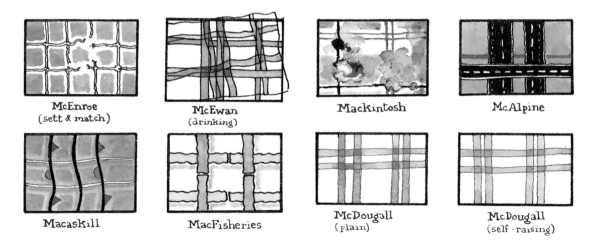

McEnroe
(sett & match)

McEwan
(drinking)

Mackintosh

McAlpine

Macaskill

MacFisheries

McDougall
(plain)

McDougall
(self-raising)

The Clan System worked relatively well for a while, but, as so often happens in families, feuds grew up over the centuries. This was known as the Feuding System.

Intense rivalry and ill-feeling (such as that between Edinburgh and Glasgow) led to constant turbulence in the Highlands. The merest clash of tartans was enough to cause the clan chief to 'send round the fiery cross', summoning the clansmen into action against the neighbours. It was a grim chapter in Scottish History.

Eventually, relations became so bad between certain clans (the Campbells and the Stewarts, the Macdonalds and the Campbells, the Campbells and the Macgregors . . .) that the government banned the wearing of tartans and Highland Costume altogether. This drastic measure exposed many to untold suffering in the harsh climate of Scottish winters.

When clothes were allowed back on again, the few remaining Scots fared little better. When kilts were made all the rage in the 19th century (being easier to make than trews), it was discovered that each kilt required 21 yards of material (or 8¾ sheep laid end to end). From this point on, people were shoved out by sheep.

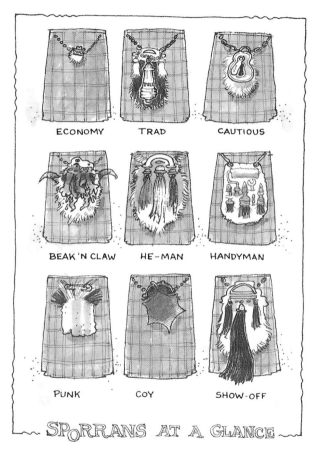

ECONOMY TRAD CAUTIOUS

BEAK 'N CLAW HE-MAN HANDYMAN

PUNK COY SHOW-OFF

SPORRANS AT A GLANCE

HIGHLAND DRESS

Highland Dress is held up traditionally by strict regulations and several large safety-pins. Contravention of the rules can lead to severe punishments, including public humiliation in the case of forfeiture of an offending item of apparel.

Those wishing to don tartan must first prove their manhood by submitting to a series of rigorous probes into their ancestry (and sometimes even exposure of their antecedents) in one of a number of Edinburgh stores specially licensed for the purpose.

Non-clanmembers tempted into the purchase of a tie should take due heed of these warnings.

Safety note: Persons wishing to don Highland Dress should never attempt this operation at a distance less than 8ft. from the nearest person

'Well fancy that, Mr Ballgladder!'

GLENGARRY
for essential
writing materials

PLAID
for picnics

ANORAK
trad.

JABOT
for wiping
porridge
off
chin

SPORRAN
for holding
golf-tees

CLAYMORE
for cutting
shortbread

SGIAN DHU
emergency
release
in case of
overtight
garters

BANDAGE LEGGINGS
to protect against
nasty accidents
during sword-dance

37

Balmoral

Deerstalker

My Bonnet
Lies over the Ocean

The Rest & Be Thankful
(Safety Model)

THE CORRECT FORM OF HIGHLAND DRESS

Great Scots: Science & Discovery

Inventors, explorers & the pioneer spirit

A wee spark
Maks muckle wark.

> (Trans. 'A young inventor in the house
> means a lot of tidying up.')

Scots have been at the forefront of many of the world's great technological breakthroughs – penicillin, the telephone bell, the Tay Bridge, the umbrella, the mackintosh . . .

For hundreds of years Scots led lives of gloomy isolation, hemmed in by wet weather in the glens. When the Industrial Revolution came along, it was only natural that Scotland's main contributions to invention and discovery should be in the field of communications – thanks to men like Thomas Telford, the creator of bridges and new towns; Kirkpatrick Macmillan, inventor of the bicycle pedal; James Watt (light-bulbs) and 'Yogi' Baird (television).

Steam was all the rage and almost overnight the sparkling waters of the Clyde were transformed into a major shipyard, fit for a Queen. (Incidentally, it is still possible to ride on the Waverley, Sir Walter Scott's pedal-boat, which to this day plies over his beloved Katrine.)

'EUREKA – I'VE INVENTED THE CYCLE-CLIP!'

When Macmillan pedalled out of his smithy on a mechanical horse, his brave action brought in its wake a succession of pioneering achievements. First Dunlop created the bicycle pump; next he came up with the inflatable tyre. Then along came Macadam with his patent new system for smoothing the roads – which development inevitably led on to the invention of the Dundee Cake.

With this rapid improvement in the roads, it now became possible for Scots to go out and explore the world – and, among explorers, there is none so famous as the great Dr. Livingstone (who discovered Mungo Park and large parts of Africa nobody knew about).

Scottish doctors became famous throughout the world, though, after Livingstone, they tended to stick together in pairs – Lister and Simpson, Cameron and Finlay, Burke and Hare.

In the footsteps of Livingstone many followed; the Scots are great adventurers. Aided by the selfless encouragement of Highland landlords, Scots have wandered the whole world over. Thus it is that even in the most remote corners of the globe the sound of the pipes may be heard on Burns Nicht, as members of the local Caledonian Society set about celebrating the homeland.

Scots abroad : Burns Nicht in the New Hebrides

'THE SCOTS ARE GREAT ADVENTURERS'

Land of Poetry & Song

Literature – The Stage – Music & Art

Speed bonnie boat like a bird on the wing
Over the sea to Skye,
There's a cloud coming down and I've things on the line
How will they ever get dry . . .

Trad.

Mention Scottish Poetry and most people will think first of the Great McGonagall, whose undoubted brilliance and originality should not, however, be allowed to outshine the accomplishments of such worthy rivals for the bardic laurel as Burns, Scott, Hogg, the Catterick Shepherd – to name but four.

It was Burns, with his unfailing insight and characteristic wit, who gave us such lines as 'A man's a man for a' that' and the immortal 'Shouldauldacquaintance beef or got'.

There are monuments and memorials to Burns all over the Lowlands and those of a literary persuasion may like to follow the Burns Trail, thoughtfully prepared by the Scottish Tourist Board for people wishing to visit the various places where Burns is buried.

Burns shares with Robert the Bruce the distinction of having been accorded more than one last resting-place (cf. 'My Heart's in the Highlands', written posthumously in 1797).

ROBERT BURNS TRYING TO THINK OF SOMETHING THAT RHYMES WITH DOON.

41

HARRY LAUDER

HARRY LAUDER
(contd)

STOP YER TICKLIN', JOCK

THE ENTERTAINERS

'Jane,' said I, 'you're looking smart,
could you masticate a tart?'
She smiled a smole near broke my heart
the lass o' Killiecrankie.

Harry Lauder

Contrary to the dour image often put across, Scotland has long been one of the world's great providers of comedy and masters of mirth – Harry Lauder, Will Fyffe, Jimmy Knapp, Lulu and the Wee Frees . . . the list could go on for ever, taking us up to the present day with the one and only Big Yeti himself, Billy Connery.

If the great days of Scottish entertainment belong to music-hall and the Glasgow Empire, it is to television that we must look for their modern counterpart. Skye TV, Opportunity Knox, the Glenrothes advert – with its many pioneering achievements, popular shows and widely networked series, Scottish television has earned itself a reputation over the years as forcing-ground for very special talents.

THE SCOTTISH PLAY: A SUMMARY
With footnotes.

Scotland has one play[1]: The Scottish Play, an Hysterical Tragedy by Shakespeare, featuring Macbeth, his dog Macduff and the Monster of Glamis. Macbeth, Thane of Glamis, is on his way home from battle when he is caught up in traffic on the heath by 3 ghastly Witches, who use unsavoury ingredients to predict what will happen in the rest of the play.

Macbeth duly becomes Thane of Cawdor and murders Duncan, but goes inthane. Banquo gets bumped off and the thane thing happens all over again. Lady Macbeth, meanwhile, is having trouble with her dog ('Out, damned Spot!') and kills herself. Macbeth decides to take all the dogs out for a walk on the blasted heath ('Lead on, Macduff!'[2]); but then he finds that, instead of walking to the trees, the trees (or Birnam Woods) are walking to him.

The play ends on a more cheerful note with Macbeth's head being cut off and given to the new king, Malcolm.

[1] apart from Peter Pan, which doesn't count.
[2] everyone knows this is the correct version, but still some editors persist with the erroneous, 'Lay on, Macduff!' – which would be a silly thing say to a dog.

GREAT WRITERS

Scotland has had many long novelists, notably Scott ('Great God! this is an awful place.'), many of whose titles have been read and enjoyed all over the world.

Other great writers include Boswell, who followed Johnson around; Carlyle, just over the Border; Conan Doyle, creator of the immortal defective; John Buchan, who originated the script for the film The 39 Steps – not to mention the great Scot Fitzgerald.

But surely the best-loved of all Scottish authors remains Robert Louis Stevenson (Kidnapped, Treasure Island, Rocket, The Black Arrow etc.). Few people know that Stevenson actually based his tale of Dr Jekyll and Mr Hyde on the real-life story of an Edinburgh magistrate, Deacon Brodie (father of Miss Jean).

THE IMPRESSIVE FRONT OF ABBOTSFORD, BUILT TO HOUSE THE WAVERLEY NOVELS.

No survey of Letters, however brief, would be complete without some reference to the part played by papers and journals in Scotland ever since the golden days of Blackwood's Magazine and the Edinburgh Revue.

The great traditions of the press are upheld to this day by the powerful D. C. Thomson Organisation in Dundee – as befits the city of 'jute, jam and journalism'.

DR JOHNSON WITH HIS FAITHFUL COMPANION ON THEIR TOUR OF THE HIGHLANDS

MUSIC

In the musical field Scotland is famous chiefly for the bagpipe, an instrument that has been sadly neglected by composers down the years. Little in the way of serious chamber-music has been written in recent times – barring the occasional, rather banal, 19th century nocturne or lullaby. Sadly, therefore, it is the case that bagpipe-players are often reduced to desperate measures for survival – banding together to play in large groups on the streets of the capital in a bid to make a livelihood for their calling.

Perhaps one reason for the rarity of bagpipe-compositions lies in the difficulties associated with prac-tising this instrument (banned in built-up areas and Sites of Special Scientific Interest). These prohibitions are generously waived by the City of Edinburgh during the month of August, when aspiring pipers are allowed to congregate around the Castle for massed practice-sessions after nightfall.

The bagpipe is essentially an instrument of the Low-lands. Travel north, around the Highlands and Islands, to enjoy the delightful sound of a Scotsman on the fiddle.

THE EARLIEST KNOWN
FORM OF BAGPIPE

A COMMON ERROR WITH
LEARNER-PIPERS

THE VISUAL ARTS

You might be forgiven for supposing that Scotland's foremost painters would have looked first to the grandeurs of Highland Scenery for subject-matter and artistic inspiration. But in fact the great names in Scottish art-circles (Ramsay, Raeburn, Raphael Tuck . . .) all made their reputations as portrait-painters, choosing to grapple with their subjects in the relative warmth and privacy of a studio.

All this changed with the arrival of Charles Rennie Mackintosh, that most versatile of innovators, who first came up with a form of waterproof clothing that made painting outdoors a possibility in Scotland – and then went one better by inventing Modern Art (or 'Art Nouveau', as he sensibly called it), which made sketching and drawing all quite unnecessary anyway. All this while still at school in Glasgow! It did not take long for his fellow-pupils to cotton on to these ideas and today the galleries of Glasgow and Edinburgh are filled with many fine examples of modern art from Scotland (as shown below).

Self-portrait after
a game of Shinty
by Vincent McGough.

'Composition II'
by
Piet Hoots Mondrian.

'Campbell's Soup Can'
by
Andy Stewart Warhol

A Sporting Nation

Golf – Skiing – Fishing – Highland Games – Great Outdoors

Sport is taken most seriously in Scotland and any visitor tempted, for example, into making an ill-advised remark at a curling-event, does so at his peril.

Team-games are well-supported in Scotland and in football the national side has a memorable record, coming second on numerous occasions.

TOURIST TIP –

When in the vicinity of a golf-course, do not hesitate to applaud warmly and call out words of encouragement and advice to golfers on the links, who will appreciate your friendly interest.

GOLF IS PLAYED EVERYWHERE IN SCOTLAND

Plentiful rough and an abundance of natural hazards have long made Scotland the ideal home for Golf.

An abundance of natural hazards...

First played by St. Andrew, the Royal and Ancient Game has been enjoyed by Kings and Queens down through the centuries. Mary Q. of Scots was a particularly keen player and is reputed to have given her executioner at Fotheringay in 1587 a few words of advice on his swing.

Today the game is played in all parts of Scotland and it is not unusual, especially around the middle of August, to see long lines of caddies patiently combing the hillsides, looking for lost balls in he heather.

Other popular sports in Scotland include shinty (a faster form of golf), swimming, football, rugby, horse-racing and fitba.

There are various forms of winter-sport, devised for keeping warm during the chillier months, and curling (or Elgin Marbles) for the less energetic.

Watch out for cricket being played in some of the more remote glens (summer months only), but in many parts the traditional game has been edged out in favour of Highland Games (see p. 54).

SHINTY – A PRE-SEASON FRIENDLY ON SKYE

A MILD JANUARY IN GLENSHEE

SPORT ALWAYS ATTRACTS A GOOD FOLLOWING IN SCOTLAND

THE ORIGINS OF CABER-TOSSING

HIGHLAND GAMES

First set up by clan chiefs keen to bring more tourism into their areas, the Highland Games have flourished beyond all expectations. The first Games grew up around those activities traditionally enjoyed by crofters, to while away the long winter evenings – piping, tug o' war, pillow-fights . . . But some of these sports have been superseded in recent years by more contemporary pursuits, such as Spotting the Beer Tent and Trying to Find Somewhere to Park.

Music and Dance are central to these sporting gatherings and competition can be ferocious among the teams assembled for All-in Formation Dancing, while the festive spirit is bravely maintained by relays of pipers (an' a' an' a') from the Grimond School of Piping, who play lamentable pieces late into the long, light nights.

View down Loch Tummel

THE GREAT OUTDOORS

For the hardy and active Scotland offers countless challenges. Downhill cycling and white-water poohsticks are just two of the many outdoor pursuits for which the landscape of Scotland seems tailor-made.

There are possibilities galore for climbing, walking, hill-running, blisters, wayfaring, pony-trekking, mule-trains, water-skiing, windsurfing, canoeing, orienteering . . . in short, a hundred and one different ways of getting lost.

As well as waymarked forest-trails, Scotland now has several excellent long-distance footpaths. The first of these to be opened was The West Highland Way, pioneered by a motorist in 1980 who set off south from Ben Nevis in search of a 'phone-box. The West Highland Way ends just outside Glasgow.

55

WALKING THE WEST HIGHLAND WAY . . .

A WORD ON MIDGES

The much-loved midge has had something of a bad press lately, notwithstanding the key role it played in the origins of the Highland Fling.

The midge is basically a shy creature, rarely encountered, indeed something of a delight to behold on the wing in the still air of a summer's evening.

Midge-bites can of course be most tiresome, but it may be as well to remember that these occur at only one time of year (the holiday season). Furthermore, midges themselves will be found only in parts of Scotland where there is water. Finally, it is only the female midge that bites. Needless irritation can therefore be avoided by the simple expedient of approaching only the male of the species.

The Midge

PONY-TREKKING ON SHETLAND

Made in Scotland

Scottish Economy – Scotch – Hydro-Electrics – Farming

SCOTTISH ECONOMY

Scotland's great financial institutions have traditionally been based in the Golden Mile along the shores of Loch Lomond ('Yon bonny banks'), a pleasant setting which still plays host to commercial venturers of every kind.

In terms of heavy industry, Scotland's days as shipbuilder of the world are sadly over, and present-day visitors are more likely to find consignments of macramé, candlework and interesting little items in antler and heather launched down the slipways of the Clyde. Scotland's foremost industry today is the manufacture of coffee-mugs. Other products include socks, North Sea oil and Scotch Tape (made in France).

A Nation at Work –
Many of Scotland's workshops throw open their doors to the public and visitors to Scotland often come for the sheer pleasure of watching others work. There is something for everyone to see – from the winding of transformer coils in Edinburgh to the butchery of venison in Auchtermuchty. You can watch heather grow in Dunoon or perhaps you would prefer to follow the Whisky Trail round Grampian before calling in for a glimpse of electricity from the viewing galleries at Pitlochry or Hunterston 'B'. There's so much to do when it rains!

SCOTCH WHISKY

UISGHIQUEGURGLHIC BAUGHURGH (Gael.) . . . The Water of Life. Legend has it that it was St. Patrick who first converted the Scotch, initiating his many followers into the precious rites of distilling. Whoever it was that first divulged the mysteries of the spirit, Scotch whisky continues to occupy a very special place in the homes and hearts of the people.

Whisky is of course still produced in the traditional way, in lofts and bathrooms throughout the Highlands and Islands. A set of bagpipes, filled with barley mash, is plumbed into the peat-fired water-heating system and allowed to gurgle away in peace for several years, its magic to perform.

Visitors wishing to unravel more of the secrets of this process should join a guided tour of one of the many distilleries, where it is possible to view a large number of different containers and pipes (as shown overleaf).

Note: While certain distilleries allow groups in to view the full process of whisky-making, others confine their visitors just to certain stages – blending, bottling etc. However, since the full process can take anything up to 15 years in the case of a prized malt, those wishing to see the whole thing through from start to finish are well-advised to make special arrangements before embarking on their visit.

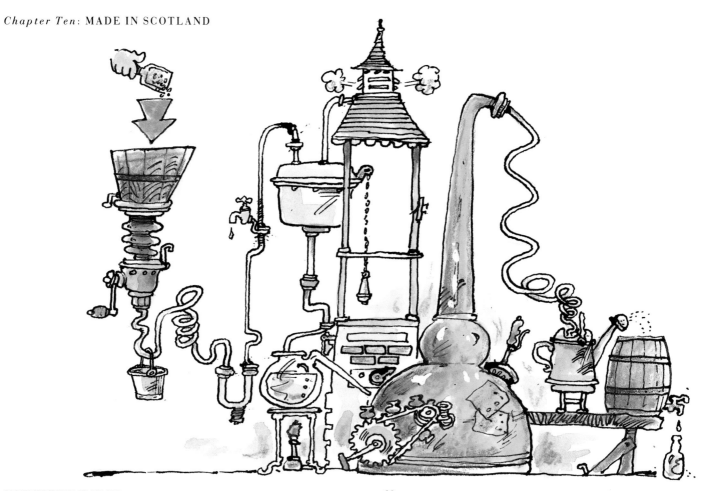

WHISKY-TASTING: THE CORRECT APPROACH

While the connoisseur may learn to tell apart a hundred and one near-identical whiskies from the merest glance at the details given on the label, the beginner is faced with an apparently impossible task when trying to choose a Scotch. A few simple rules may assist:

1) Always look first at the price.
2) The character of a Scotch may best be ascertained by holding the glass close to one's ear and listening out for its special 'ring'.

3) NEVER ever swallow your whisky: it should first be rolled around the mouth and then expelled discreetly into one of the decorated ice-buckets provided in all bars for this purpose.
4) Remember, it is the peat in the water that gives the whisky its distinctive colour. Consequently some of the best Scotch whiskies are to be found in regions where the water is particularly brown and full of body.

5) Learn to distinguish between two basic types of whisky, blended and single malt – but do not be afraid to ask for unleaded, now obtainable in most areas.
6) Finally, do always watch out for the age on the label and don't let yourself be fobbed off with old stock well past its best.

... full of body ...

HYDRO-ELECTRICS EXPLAINED

The economy of Scotland relies heavily on tourism, which is in turn dependent on the weather – a few good summers can play havoc with the tourist figures, as disappointed holidaymakers stay away in their droves, unwilling to gamble on Scotland without the mist and rain they've been led to expect.

It is therefore of vital importance to Scotland's well-being that a steady flow of wet weather is maintained across the country – this in an age of global warming and major climatological change. Bearing in mind also the continuing great processes of geological metamorphosis (the slow rise of the Caledonian land-mass, the constant removal of gemstones by craft workshops and the steady erosion of rock-features by school-parties with geologist's hammers), it is easy to understand the anxieties of experts concerned with Scotland's future.

Haunted by the spectre of a Scotland without water (sun-parched uplands; lochs drained, all but for a stagnant sludge thick with midge larvae; not to mention the dire consequences that would befall an empty Loch Ness . . .), the authorities have set about implementing a bold scheme to maintain the fragile eco-system of Scotland's inheritance.

In a clever arrangement of straegically placed installations, electric-power is used to drive the pumps and wheels that turn the waters to keep the rivers flowing, the burns fed and a constant supply of mist in the air. This is the famous Hydro-Electric Scheme of Scotland.

FARMING

Traditional farming still plays an important part in the Scottish economy – indeed much of the population of the Highlands and Islands is made up of fishermen and small farmers.

Produce and methods vary greatly with the climate. Potatoes are the staple-crop of the Lowlands and much

"Fishermen and small farmers ..."

ingenuity goes into developing new strains of seed-potato – red, white, pink and even tartan (Murdoch).

Over in the east of Scotland are frost-free zones which favour the growing of soft-fruit – though a new variety of ready-frozen raspberry is now at the experimental stage in the Cairngorms. Between Forth and Tay lies Fife, world-famous for bananas.

Adverse weather conditions make farming a tough proposition in the extreme north of Scotland, where the land is generally too wet and the soil too poor for conventional methods of cultivation. However, a major development in recent years has been the sudden proliferation of fish-farming, which has proved something of a growth industry in the Highlands.

"... something of a growth industry ..."

① BELTED GALLOWAY
(half Ayrshire
half panda)

② HIGHLAND (front)   (rear)

③ AYRSHIRE
CROSS

④ FREEZIAN
(milk high in
ice-cream content)

⑤ ABERDEEN FUNGUS

CATTLE BREEDS OF SCOTLAND

Members of the Strathclyde Serious Crimes Squad Cattle-Reiving Patrol
on active duty in the Highlands of Scotland

Sheep-farming is carried on in all parts, an enterprise that owes much of its success to selective-breeding and the development over the years of a special Scottish non-shrink variety of sheep. In the Outer Hebrides this hardy breed is fed on a diet supplemented with fishmeal – hence Harris Tweed herringbone. Meanwhile at the top secret Sheep Research Station on Rhum, scientists are working on the 'shebra', a Cheviot/Polyester crossbreed carrying genes of the zebra, with a view to creating the perfect fleece in ready-printed tartan.

Rhum Crossbreed

Traditional methods of
cattle transport

Finally cows, without which no account of Scottish farming would be complete. The coarse pastures of the uplands give dairy products in Scotland a certain tenacity and resilience, as shown by the superb dunlop cheeses of Gigha. Nonetheless, Highland Cattle today lead rather duller lives than those of their Victorian counterparts. In the course of their final journey to a last roasting-place in times gone by, Highland cattle swam the Minches, trod the Caledonian drove-roads, were rustled by night, hidden in mountain-corries, scaled vertical cliffs and covered the length and breadth of the A1, before reaching Smithfield, where they were at last well and truly knackered. Scotch Beef has a reputation for leanness with a slightly salty tang and occassional blisters.

HIGHLAND TERRIFIER

WEE CAIRNS

GREYFRIARS BOBBY

BORED COLLIE

SCOTTISH DOG-BREEDS

The Way of Life

Hame's Hame – Politics & Religion – Natural Character

HAME'S HAME A SCOTSMAN'S HOME

Alas, poverty does still exist in Scotland, with large families sharing cold and discomfort in forbidding and gloomy tenements like that pictured alongside.

Of course, not all Scots have had to face the grinding burden of struggling to maintain an ancient building; at the time of the famous Clearances, many Scots suddenly found themselves free to start up new homes in attractive seaside locations – a policy which found favour both with the Dukes of Sutherland in their castle of Dunrobbin' and with the sheep, who became new owners of interesting properties in the Highlands.

Often all that remains now of these properties is a heap of stones and the rowan-tree always planted in the past to ward off evil spirits. Some people still keep up this delightful tradition by placing outside their home a jar or two of home-made rowan jelly, which will keep off most things.

INSIDE A CROFT

Hardship is not new to Highland folk and the canny Scot has always been able to make a virtue out of necessity, as can be seen from this charming view of a traditional crofter's interior –

Nowadays such properties are eagerly sought after by Museums of Rural Life and displaced persons from Surrey wishing to live with goats.

69

POLITICS AND RELIGION

Centuries of deprivation, oppression and drizzle in Scotland have done nothing to weaken the National Spirit, a steady supply of which has enabled the people to survive the rigours of a tragic past. Small wonder too, against this background, that politics and religion should play a significant role in Scottish affairs.

Over the years Scotland has been birthplace, home and refuge to many important political parties – Keir Hardie, the Liberals and even the SNP. The list of famous politicians from Scotland includes a great many ex-prime Ministers (Ramsay Macdonald, David Balfour, Macmillan, Home, the Blasted Heath . . .) and Winnie Ewing.

The Kirk
For several centuries now, Religion in Scotland has been split down the middle into two great opposing forces, Celtic and Rangers. Crowd trouble is generally held to be the root cause of religious difficulties in Scotland, probably dating back to the earlier practice of throwing stools in cathedrals, one of which broke The Covenant.

The Hirsel, hume of Lord Home

John Knox sharing a joke with friends

NATIONAL CHARACTERISTICS

The traditional image of the Scot is of someone with sandy-red hair, a thick beard and a tendency to knobbly knees. This stereotype bears little relationship to modern realities, not least in the case of women. Nowadays it is by no means unusual to find dark-haired Scots (descended from the shipwrecked mariners of the Spanish Armada).

Scots today fall into two basic types, Heelan and Loolan, and can be told apart by hairstyle:—

CELTIC FRINGE

EDINBURGH FRINGE

LANG MAY YER RUM LEAK

In Scotland there is a saying for almost everything and native Scots are much given to the quotation of proverbs and rhymes for every occasion. One small consequence of this natural sport, giving rise to some concern in government circles, is the steady growth each year in the number of lines of verse by Robert Burns.

The Celtic love of words and music is strong in Scotland, where people are hospitable by nature and like nothing better than a friendly sing-song and an excuse to let down their trousers.

A friendly sing-song...

71

Bide-A-Wee

Board & Lodging – Oat Cuisine

BOARD & LODGING

Wherever you go in Scotland, one thing is for certain: you can be sure of a homely welcome. Scots are famous for their hospitality the whole world over.

FOOD IN SCOTLAND –

Bannocks

Scotland, home of Chop Soay and the Big Mac, is of course no stranger to the world of international cuisine and the fast-food takeaway.

But it is home cooking and traditional fare for which Scotland is rightly famous. Don't go making the mistake of thinking this just means porridge, porridge, oatcakes and porridge! There's drummock and farls, bannocks and crowdie, Atholl Brose, parritch and all sorts of interesting things rolled in oats.

TOURIST TIPS

1. It is normal in Scotland for most meals to be brought to the table preceded by a solitary piper. (Visitors are advised to make their own inquiries into local arrangements when booking into hotels where breakfast is served in the bedroom.)
2. Do not offend your hosts at table through ignorance of local customs. For sugar, use salt throughout.

Do not be surprised to find free-range eggs, home-made bread and marmalade, local heather honey and fresh-ground coffee all appearing on the breakfast menu

Arbroath Smokie

Oat Cuisine

As you travel around Scotland, you may stumble upon all manner of local speciality, rarely found elsewhere – neeps and tatties, for example, or even Scotch Egg. Watch out for freshly poached salmon and, if in season, a newly-bagged cock-a-leekie, cullen skink or Scotch woodcock straight off the moors.

Each region has its own mouthwatering dishes – Forfar Bridies, Arbroath Smokies and so on. On Shetland you can enjoy krappin, wirtiglugs, snoddie and slot.

Elsewhere in Scotland, the menu for a very special meal out might read as follows:–

Starters: MELLON UDRIGLE, BEINN EIGHE or
LARGS
Main Course: LENA ZAVARONI, GOLSPIE or
TOMINTOUL
Sweets: RHUM EIGG MUCK, GROATIE BUCKIES or
CHOICE OF TARBETS.

TOURIST TIPS

1. The correct way to eat porridge is with a spirtle, usually available on request in most good hotels and B&B (bothy & bannock) establishments.
2. Eating venison can pose quite a problem in polite circles. First detach the antlers and leave these discreetly by the side of your plate.

ENTERTAINMENTS

Customs, ceilidhs & Places to Visit

LOCAL CUSTOMS

Christmas doesn't often happen in Scotland, but Hogmanay (to celebrate the arrival of Andy Stewart) is a great occasion, when people rise in the night, dressed in white heather, and dance round their friends – bringing them good luck by being the first to step on their feet.

A favourite pastime of all Scots is the 'ceilidh' – an informal get-together, when folk can meet over a glass for a quiet shindig. Rest assured, wherever you stay in Scotland, there will be a ceilidh not too far away – usually in the room below.

A FEW DATES FOR YOUR DIARY

January 25 – Burns Night

January 26 – Haggis Leftovers

January   – Up-Helly-Aa: festival of rapine and pillage in Lerwick.

February – Ba Game in Jedburgh (Borders): arrival of the first holiday caravan.

June   – Grampian Goat Show

July   – Sheepdog Trials Quarter Sessions in Strathbogie

August   – Federation of Scottish Plumbers meet in Dunoon for National Piping Contest.

September – Fiddle & Accordian Club Gala Week on Canna.

October   – National Mod: rally and events.

HOW TO DANCE THE NADGERS O' DOON

Traditional Reel for 3 couples and a cat.

① First couple poussette, cast off, set to and come to blows.

② as per diagram.

③ Attempt to disentangle. If not possible, send for Fire Brigade.

Diagram:

A chance encounter between new-style deerstalkers and members of the Strathclyde Anti-Reiving Patrol on a dark night in the Highlands...

PLACES TO VISIT: THINGS TO DO

Suggested Tours:
i) Castles in Ayr
Scotland positively brims with castles to visit, some of them (like Glamis) still inhabited by their original owners. For a castle with a difference, why not pop into Culzean, begun in 1777, and therefore of considerable historical significance, being one of the few castles not visited by Mary, Queen of Scots.

Those interested in pursuing this fascinating sideline on History, should ask at any Information Centre for the slim leaflet 'Places of Interest Not Slept In By Mary Queen of Scots'.

ii) Island-Hopping
There are 786 offshore islands around Scotland and 498 at low tide. Of course, not all of these are inhabited today; some, like the Summer Isles, are visible only from May to September, while one or two others are towed into sheltered ports for the winter months.

An interesting time can be had working out a suitable route to enable you to cover all the islands in the course of your holiday. Try the Fishing Heritage Trail, from Fishnish to Vaternish, calling in at Trotternish, Mishnish, Fishdish and Treshnish (unsuitable for those with speech impediments).

TOURIST TIP
Do not be surprised to find night-clubs and gaming establishments closed on Sundays, particularly along the more remote stretches of the West Coast and Islands.

iii) Grampian Wild Goose Trail

This is an ideal tour for those with a little extra money to spend.

From the Roadside of Kinneff, follow the Path of Condie, avoiding Spittal of Glenshee wherever possible. Continue by Carse of Gowrie to Port of Monteith, where you can catch the Boat of Garten for a round tour of the Pool o' Muckhart. Treat yourself to a slap-up stay overnight at the Hilton of Cadboll.

Other suggestions for an interesting day out might include
- hang-gliding over Balmoral
- sizzling in the sunshine on the coast of Fife (The Scottish Riviera)
- a visit to the mighty Victoria Falls at Kinlochewe, discovered by Livingstone in 1855.
- a chance meeting with the great birks of Aberfeldy
- paying a call on the grave of Rob Roy in Balquhidder churchyard.

VISITING ROB ROY'S GRAVE

FOR FURTHER READING:
What's On in Foula
Tie Your Own Flies
1001 Things To Do in Achiltibuie
Enjoy Scotland Or Else (pack)

On the Road

A Round Tour – Motoring Advice – Bridges

SCOTLAND IN PHOTOGRAPHS

No it's not a Hebridean sunset - that's just the beginning of the film ...

This is a loch ...

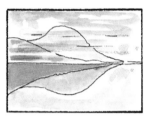

... or was it this way round?

And this is another loch. Actually that's a seal by that rock, that little dot -

or we think it may have been an otter - hard to tell as it didn't really move while we were there ...

Oh, that's one from the wedding that shouldn't be in with this lot ...

<u>Technical Note</u>: Pictures taken on a Junior Instamatic at £7.99, with wrist-strap facility, using a free film from Boots, with the stop on Cloudy in manual operating mode.

That's one of the Cairngorms from the car window...

Pity about the weather on that one...

This was a deer we got really close to (in a Wildlife Park)

Actually, I didn't take this one - it's one of those Colin Baxter cards we sent everyone. See, he didn't get very good weather either...

Now this I'm really pleased with. It was an incredible sunset...

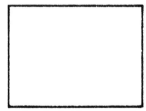

...typical: this was when the pine marten nipped my toe while I was watching the two eagles soar over Kintail beneath the rainbow and I'd just run out of film...

MOTORING ADVICE

Driving in Scotland can be hazardous. Before setting out, make sure that you are properly acquainted with the following road-signs –

Haggis on road

Number of miles to next filling-station

Ceilidh ahead

Straighter bit of road ahead

Tea Shoppe ahead

You are now crossing the Highland Fault

Tartan Mill Shop Ahead

Bagpipe practice area

Watch out for detachments of Japanese with guns

THE CORRECT PROCEDURE WHEN TWO VEHICLES MEET ON A SINGLE-TRACK ROAD AT AN EQUAL DISTANCE FROM PASSING-PLACES

1. Groan.

2. Signal your intentions clearly to the oncoming vehicle...

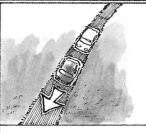

3. Begin to reverse.

4. Observe car ahead now also reversing. Go forward again

5. On seeing car ahead now also coming forward, re-commence reverse.

6. Hit bloody van that's just crept up on your rear without any warning.

7. Begin again at (1) above...

THE UNIQUE CHARACTER OF SCOTLAND'S ROAD NETWORK
CAN GIVE RISE TO PROBLEMS NOT ENCOUNTERED ELSEWHERE...

BRIDGES

Scotland is held together by bridges, many of them justly famous – Bridge of Orchy, Bridge of Cally, Brig o' Doon, the Rumbling Bridge in Devon, the Forth Bridges, the Bridge over the Atlantic . . .

Most of these were built single-handed by General Wade in a fit of pique, on hearing from the ranks one too many taunts on his name, when marching his men round Scotland in the 18th century.

The Outer Hebrides are now joined up by a system of bridges and causeways (The Road to the Isles), making it possible to motor the full way from Barra Head to Butt of Lewis – a pleasant drive when the tide is out.

JOHN O' GROATS-TO-LANDS END CHARITY-WALKER
PASSING LANDS END-TO-JOHN O' GROATS
CHARITY-WALKER JUST SOUTH OF JOHN O' GROATS.

The Language

Glossary – Names – Pronunciation – Vocabulary

Most Scots speak Erse, but in the north and west Gaelic may still be heard. Gaelic (pronounced 'Gall-ic') is a form of French dating back to the Auld Alliance.

Where English is spoken, it may be with considerable variations of accent and dialect, according to region and time on a Saturday night.

GLOSSARY:

bairn	– large outbuilding
birk	– short dagger
bonspiel	– great skua
bonxie	– curling match
caddie	– smoked haddock
corbie	– new town
corrie	– cream cheese
crowdie	– large crow
dirk	– birch tree
girdle	– griddle
griddle	– girdle

haddie	– golf attendant
hinnie	– water demon
kelpie	– sweetheart
lug	– chimney
lum	– ear
neuk	– coastal polaris base
sassenach	– sausage
sassenger	– English person
sika	– type of pine-tree
sitka	– type of deer
tattoo	– potato
wabbit	– long-eared wodent

FINNAN CADDIE

NAMES

Surnames in Scotland can prove a trap for the unwary (and a nightmare for users of the telephone directory).

As a general rule, it is safe to pronounce only the first, middle and last letters of any surname plus a maximum of two further letters IF THE TOTAL NUMBER OF LETTERS IN THE NAME EXCEEDS EIGHT.

Thus, DALYELL, RUTHVEN, COLQUHOUN and BUCCLEUCH become DYL, RVN, CLUN and BCLUH.

When it comes to difficult vowel-sounds (Maclean, Macleod, McVean etc.), the golden rule is always to move the 'e' back to the end of the word and drop the voice on the last syllable.

Recurrent difficulties over pronunciation of surnames, let alone forenames, explain why some families have tended to drop names altogether, in favour of a return to an older system of generic plant-labelling (The MacNab, The Macleod of Macleod, Moncrieff of that Ilk and so on).

TOURIST TIP

A great many people in Scotland are called 'Jimmy', especially in the Glasgow area; however, first-time visitors may feel happier using the more formal 'James' when addressing virtual strangers.

"Ah, elevingis!"

SCOTTISH PRONUNCIATION: ADULT EVENING CLASS IN FULL FLOW...

WORDS FROM SCOTLAND: SOME USEFUL VOCABULARY

Helpful Information

What to Wear – Key to symbols – Conversion Charts

WHAT TO WEAR

Clothing is recommended in all parts of Scotland, though provision is made for naturists in designated areas around Wick and the north coast of Sutherland. Watch out for the charming Thistle Sign, indicating the presence of a nudist beach nearby.

It is customary to dress for dinner in Scotland, donning as many layers of clothing as the draughtiness of the surroundings require. Stout footwear, ideally waterproof, is a must at all times. If in any doubt, slip on a pair of galoshes before setting out on any venture.

Otherwise, do feel free to dress casually, as you would at home – except on Sundays, when it is required by law in certain areas for black to be worn.

TOURIST TIP
It is considered extremely rude to look in someone else's sporran.

The Antrim Coast seen from the Mull of Kintyre

TOURIST FACILITIES:

KEY TO SYMBOLS –

♘ cycle-clip repairs undertaken

♠ dog toilet

🎿 area exposed to high winds

☺ emergency tailoring on hand

☕ pots in all bedrooms

⚔ free-range Highland Dancing

📺 television not working

🦌 Christmas Shopping Centre

🏰 not another Heritage Centre

CONVERSION CHARTS

SCOTTISH   —   ENGLISH

Distances:
1 mile   —   4¾ miles (7.64275 km)
no far   —   several miles
a wee way   —   several more miles

Liquids:
a dram   —   ¼ pint (14.2057 cl)
a wee drap   —   ½ pint (28.4115 cl)

Currency:
1 poond   —   98.37 pence

The Mull of Kintyre seen from the Antrim Coast

Land of Secrets

Scotched Myths

Scotland has Three Great Secrets, about which so much has already been said and written that these are in grave danger of remaining secret no more.

These final pages provide just a brief glimpse into the private, dark worlds of Loch Ness, the Haggis and what goes on under a Scotsman's kilt –

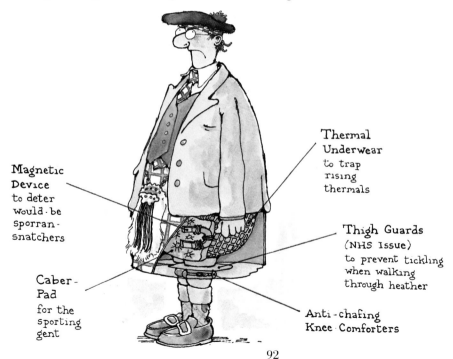

Magnetic Device to deter would-be sporran-snatchers

Caber-Pad for the sporting gent

Thermal Underwear to trap rising thermals

Thigh Guards (NHS Issue) to prevent tickling when walking through heather

Anti-chafing Knee Comforters

Rutting haggis caught in the headlights of a southbound kipper lorry...

...a victim of the growing traffic problem in the Highlands: an ex-haggis ready to make an important contribution to Scotland's Sporran Industry.

WINTER SQUALL BRINGING FRUSTRATION TO MEMBERS OF THE LOCH NESS SURVEY TEAM

INDEX

Haste ye back!